Cleared for Landing

"Look if you like but you will have to leap."
W.H. Auden

Cleared
for
Landing
POEMS BY
Ann Darr

DRYAD PRESS

Washington, D.C. and San Francisco

Acknowledgements
Some of these poems have appeared or will appear
in the following journals: *The New Republic,
The Carleton Miscellany, Choice, The Paris Review,
Dryad, The Chowder Review, Caim, Poetry Now,
The Washington Review of the Arts, The Salt Lick
Press, Black Box, Sojourner, Squeezebox, Criterion,
Red Clay Reader, The Portland Review, Hampden-
Sydney Review.* "The Argument" first appeared in
Three Rivers Journal, copyright © 1975
by Three Rivers Press.

The author wishes to express her gratitude to the
National Endowment for the Arts for a literary fellowship
which provided the time for writing several of these poems.

DRYAD PRESS

P.O. Box 1656
Washington, D.C. 20013

2943 Broderick Street
San Francisco, California 94123

PS
3554
.A73
C 5

For George

Contents

What Shall We Say to Our Sister?

THE ARGUMENT

I am writing an order to L L Bean.
I need a hair shirt and two
well-seamed apologies and their factory
up in Freeport, or down Maine,
is the only one I know that stays open
all night. Maybe I should telephone.
Person to shirt. Dear Friend. No logic
lodged in that fight we had. We
were suddenly hard-eyed and yelling
over nothing that concerned us
in the living lode. It came on
fast like a summer storm from
a direction we weren't looking.
I thought we could turn back but
the bridge was down. Weeks have
ended and there is only a dry
telephone voice...no, I am not
coming...am not interested. And interest
was all I ever had. Somewhere I knew it was
a luxury, shouting at you. I've tried
to reason it out, but reason
was never a route to approach you by.
I was angry for all women against
all men. I was angry because you
had found the escape route. Which
meant you would never again need
comfort from me. And that was
the name of the bridge.

IT IS THE BREATHING

Nine hundred miles away I hear the breathing.
Under the oxygen, the little flippety door
moves open and shut, open and shut.
It is the breathing that keeps her alive
and somewhere under the lonely tick of the clock
the air comes on like muffling comforters.

She is standing at the window
gasping for air she breathed in
90 years ago. She hears the wind
in her ears but the leaves hang limp.
They are calling her to come over, come over.

She steps out the window onto the keyboard
of the old Knabe grand. Its leaves, its grapes,
its lion feet uphold her. Now the river
is running through Grand Street
and on her piano raft, she floats away.

INSIGHT NUMBER 76

Okay, Kids, you can cremate me.
The myth is over. There's not
going to be a Resurrection Day.
I didn't want to show up
as a small grey ash. I wanted
to walk in with my own body
so my friends would recognize me.
And we could do a little
singing and dancing and
living it up.
      Or was it
that I couldn't bear the thought
of not having my body to lay
on yours, sir, ever ever again.

DEAR JAMES WRIGHT,

this is a Spring I am already
troubled with. I have played
my whole hand, only to find,
as I turned over card after card,
nothing in sequence, no face
cards at all. I sit here with
a handful of clay from the river
trying to mold my face. I look
in the mirror, see nothing.
Nosebleeds, headaches indicate
something.
                    I am glad
you are on the wagon. Lengthening
your life is a good idea.

                    Once I hid
my wagon under the weeds beside
the Shenandoah when I canoed out
in winter. A week later, it was gone.
There is more thievery, murder
in the countryside than anyone wants
to believe. It's supposed to be
joy and wildflowers,
but you know about rivers—
the goddamned ever-flowing
junk-clogged rivers flowing
inside and out. If I can ever
find another wagon I ought to
climb on. All my braincells
are washing downstream. love,

DO YOU KNOW WHAT'S BETTER
THAN HAVING A MOUNTAIN
NAMED AFTER YOU?

Keep doing those Immelman turns,
she said, but I have lost track
of Immelman. Must hunt him up or
down or find the flight text
telling how to make the track
of his turn like a cat's cradle
in air, or one of those math-
ematical excitements that has
no beginning or end or any
one plane exactly like another.
Stay amazed, she said, and gave
me back my acrobatic fantasy
turning end over end
in a sky that nurtured me,
falling and feinting and climbing,
and happy as that lark whose song
may be the most beautiful sound
I have ever heard.
                   Immelman,
where are you? Where is
your moebius loop?

PASS

If my hands had murder written
in the palms, the canned cherries
would have been poison
as you thought they were.
Botulism has staggered through
the centuries answering human whistles
like a Saint Bernard.

Nothing but words can redeem us.
It's too late for words to redeem us.
Love has whittled itself a small wooden pipe
and is wandering over the hills playing child.

Only in my mind will I lie in your garden
on sheets covered with flowers,
where I have lain all these years,
killing intruders. Destroying
my fingerprints. Making elaborate maps
to lead anyone astray. Love, it is too late.
Pass on, says the guard, pass

TEMPLE ON THE BELTWAY
OPENS TO THE MEDIA

Sustained by two bloody marys
and the look of the prophet about my host,
I took my introductory letter and drove,
slowly to be sure, to miss the ceremony
and arrived in time for all but the first
angelical choir rendition. Odd.

The angel Moroni stood aghast in the sky,
   gilded and trumpeting.
How many accidents on the Beltway has he
   embellished?
Saints and brothers and Solomon's oxen of the deep,
immersed in horns and polluted waters.
O God, the mercy flowing
from the mouths of the almighty
dressed in white and seeking heaven
through timid marble mounting
seven stories and no way to see
  out or through.
Royal orchids and fecundities
trailing ambiguities,
tithes and secret smiles.
  Do not arrest me,
  officers of the state,
  silhouetted between spires,
  guns hanging out
  of your pockets,
I am aligned.
I lay down in the pastures of my God
  and was trampled by sheep.
I came to on the far side of enigma
  drenched with hot adulterous breath.
I longed for golden pinnacles,

17

doubted them all.
18,000 missionaries are somewhere else.

Dear Editor: I am alive and well
    in the garden of iniquity.
You dreamers, scanning sin,
fingering the eternal,
something here is blasphemous.

AUGUST HALLUCINATION

Of course, the horoscope said
        keep silent and you can have
        the best of both worlds, so
I kept my secret and blossomed
        in white petunias
        and queen ann's lace,
        ageratum and corn flowers
and my tongue lapped and licked
        the solid flowers of your body
and when the summer was over
        I sank in nettles and turd piles
and the glorious adventure of
        secrets had gone to seed

catalogues and unconscious itching.

Your answer was no. and I zeroed in
        to the zero. Not knowing
        you had a floating yes.

If I could hate you now, I would.
This morning's horoscope says
        good news from abroad.
        What ho! that she you covet
has said no again, I hope. Old blood
and bones, you called yourself.
        Let me go.

Talking too much, I told you too much.
Told you my love and hate,
        the abominable snowshoe
        not fitting Cinderella.
And we could laugh, the laughter
seeping through the edge of

ridiculous space, the empty luminous
    angular rotten space
    filled with ancient elbows
    and black tarnished leaves.

You came up the mountain
    through gnarled roots
    honesty, honest
as interwoven as squirrel dung
    Grandfather's bell you say
and I am clanging and you
are sitting naked in the Irish countryside
    with a lesbian on your lap
and telling me about it. I should have
cornered the market in ridiculous laughs.
    I should have cut you to shreds.

FUTURES

I wanted the future to be a surprise
and now the surprise is:
there isn't any future.

The future in sowbellies
five/eighths off.
The magnanimous curve.

My freezer is full
of red croquet balls:
frozen tomatoes.

It is not that the buttered bread
lands upside down, it is
that I always drink from the chipped side
of this glass.

Prune when the knife is sharp.
There are no seasons:
seasoning depends on metal.

For you to turn from
what I want the most,
plants an enemy
in my chest. Pandora.

THE REPLY

For Roland Flint

What shall we say to our sister?
Say that we have found a way to ground the sun,
say that we will come back over the rim of the world
and load her on our sled and travel together
forever after and she will never be lonely again,
say that.
And she will say she has broken open the egg
of the world and found it empty, and she has
climbed into the boat of the oceans and the sails
were missing, and she has listened to the cottonwood
leaves rattle their death rattle through every season
of the year, and has risen in the middle of the night
to mount the sled and the snow glistens under the moon,
the laughter freezes.
Say to our sister that she need cry no more,
we will bring buckets for tears to empty them
in the ocean so they will do no more harm
to the garden, so the salt will buoy up
our bodies instead of killing the plants, say
we have found the secret of light in Greece,
say she will never need to live without lovers,
say she will grow new bone marrow to replace the old,
say you are sorry it comes too late to do her any good,
say that.
And she will say hokuspokus, and she will say
santo domingo, aliminokus, and she will say
open sesame seed, and don't ever darken my door
again, and she will say hickory dickory dock,
my death will stop the clock, and she will say
thank you and farewell, the jig is up.

And say to our sister how her bone marrow
has blighted the garden, and hell is in her
head, how the earth is a great cereal box
with a prize inside, the Garden of Eden,
and she will say she has walked the railroad
ties searching for copperheads, she has
grabbed the axe that struck the rattles
from the rattler's tail, that she has become
sister to the snake by watching him hold his head
alert in the grass to observe the light.

Relative Matter

RELATIVE MATTER

I am writing to cancel
the invitation to come
visit us. You are not
      welcome.

We have had a volcano
erupt in the middle of
our plot of land and
      no one

has survived. The onslaught
was sudden, no warning at
all, only sudden hot shame
      pouring

over everyone. Incredulity
spilled over the mantels, light-
bulbs exploded with sudden
      insight.

We were awash with fury
and indignation. Hate
has corroded everything left
      standing.

We have only the slightest clue
as to the beginnings. Someone
mentioned your name. the way you dam-
      age things.

ON A CATOCTIN MOUNTAIN

Only once did we make love in a wild strawberry bed.
We were marking the end, or maybe a beginning.
The hill was warm and tipped the bed to the west,
we were doing our best to head in the right direction.
So if it were all contrived and like a play set,
or if it were accidental, I can't remember.
There was the faint smell of sorrow baking
in the sun, and the wonder of those berries, sweet
and reachable, even as we had just found our bodies sweet
and reachable, even then

I GAVE MY LOVE A

Once for Christmas
I gave you an accordion,
piano type. You
opened the package
and said What do I
need with a suitcase?

Once for Christmas
I gave you a windmill
used in *Mother Courage*
as scenery, but you
said it wasn't tall
enough to bring the
water up from the river.
I returned it.

Once for Christmas
I gave you a crystal
ball and you looked
into it and saw
the whole world
going blank and you
threw it as far
as friction and force
allowed and this year

I am giving you
for Christmas
a skin stretched
tight as a drum,
and a track record
even Cupid
might admire.

OBLIQUE BIRTH POEM

Labor Room: three handed
cribbage, interrupted by jack-pot
coming on. Back to the game. I win
three dollars and twenty cents...
Now!
I have never seen a birth before,
hold the mirror over here
and now in her garland of
cheese and while we are still
connected, I am towing you, my little
skiff, my boat, come into my arms,
onto my deck, sunlight has just
shone through, and the crazy doctor
bursts into song.

THE CURIOUS NIGHT
BEFORE ELIZABETH

Children are pouring
water through baskets

parachutes ripple
the sills

the women's curious
shouts of derision

huddle against
flame-colored buds

James T Farrell is
holding forth
on politics

I am about to give birth

I am about to give birth

James T Farrell is
folding the scene
into paragraphs

the women's curses,
shrieks of delirium

curdle against
flame-shaped bulbs

parachutes ruffle
the hills

children are pouring
from baskets

water is breaking

GIFTS FOR A DANCING DAUGHTER

What shall I send you? a robe
that doesn't fit. Dirndels
that dwindle. Words that waddle.
I try for philosophy and end with
advice. You ask for knives. I find
a set resembling weapons, refuse to
buy them. Buy, instead, a set that
won't cut, probably. Failures are
only important to those who are.
Now in your triumph, you gather
my depression. Nothing is ever
enough. Everything is never
enough. We mistake hunger for
love, or love for hunger.

All right! I deliver your
heritage. With all of the flukes.
I deliver the downs. I deliver
the ego, unappeased, the long blue
nightmares, the guilt. I send you
the years when the possibility
was legs called piano, was legs
stultified. I send you my panic
when the hands of the cellist
moved lightly and called through
my veins like an omen. I send
you your possible death wrapped
in tissue. I send you the carved
heart of that surgeon. I send you
your middle age. Exchange it
for dollars while you can.

2 A.M. IN THE PINEY WOODS

The children have split
and I have gone to the house on the beach
with three other dreamers
and here at 2 A.M. in the Piney Woods
my mind has leaped onto the music
and my hands dance into their grooves
and my saxophone whines in the night.

And the children have said a polite goodbye
and collected their checks
and climbed aboard airplanes
and you second dreamer
are here in the 2 A.M. in the Piney Woods
with your left heel bouncing
and your drum is booming
and your cymbals clang in the night.

And the children have breathed with relief
and waved from the window
and we are hoping the check won't bounce,
and you third dreamer
are here in the 2 A.M. in the Piney Woods
with your shoulders shaking
and your hands tattooing the keyboard
and the beat is right in the night.

And the children have forgotten us
and we have forgotten the children
and you fourth dreamer
are here in the 2 A.M. in the Piney Woods
with your slack wrists flicking,
your fingers clickclacking
and what we are making is music in the night.

THE POT-BELLIED ANACHRONISM

I have this bulging belly because:

of a deep desire for pregnancy
long past the possibility.
I wanted a baseball team, at least.

it is my anchor to this role. If
I had been trim and sleek and presentable,
I would have disappeared with every
young man who winked at me twice. This
is known as insurance. Double-bellied indemnity.

to keep my daughters from having
to compete with me, after they learn
I am more to the world than their mother.

it is the 'cross-I-bear,' the burden for
all those things I am guilty of. It will
remind me every time I fold it into my lap
that innocence has fled.

it is my feminist posture. Way out front.
Men's bellies are never regarded with derision,
snickered about, offered a girdle.

I am making a statement. That I can be any
shape I want, even pudding-shaped and
nobody can stop me.

FOLK SONG FOR AN ANNIVERSARY

It was a day like this, like any other,
the leaves had gone to Spanish colors,
past the peak of orange, the peak of yellow,
but the air was mellow enough for an open car
from Manhattan to Connecticut.

> O merry, marry, merry, marry me.

And the sky was blue,
blue as an Iowa sky.

> The best man was delayed at Bloomingdale's
> auditioning for a Santa Claus job.
> He played the role for years.

O merry, marry, merry, marry you.

> Your hands were beautiful hands
> and your eyes were luminous green
> and your laugh rang out like
> my father's laugh. Genes.

There is no such thing as love at first sight.
There is no such thing as first sight.
Light is eliptical and bends back upon itself.
I knew as soon as I saw him
I would have his children if I could.

> O merry, merry, marry, marry me.

And the dark has bent back upon itself.
If the light, then also the dark will bend.
And this is a day like any other
when the leaves have gone to Spanish colors.
Oxblood, amber, ochre, rust.

> The sky is Irish blue.
> Marry me.

35

What Are You Most Afraid Of?

WHAT ARE YOU MOST AFRAID OF?

For the Visiting Poet, Samuel Allen

What are you afraid of?
Storms, snakes, bombs.
What are you most afraid of?
My father.

Across the Maryland countryside
Mephistopheles led us in a high speed dash
up hills, around corners, swerving between
glowing yellow trees, the fires of Autumn.
Overhead huge cloud tracks cobbled the sky
with ice as we raced after the devil himself,
screeching tires, dropping our stomachs
on every angled rise. We would arrive, but where?

Ann, Ann, a farmer's lass,
Stepped on the pedal,
Stepped on the gas,
Raced the devil
Toward orchard grass
After Mephistopheles.

I who can read maps with the ends of my fingers,
upside down, out of one eye, running backward,
(twenty-thousand-eye-movements-a-second) all the dials
adjusted, poised at that maximum moment, exact
in altitude (five hundred feet, Darr, NOT 499 or
501) sweetly sweetly on the stick, ever so gently
the pressure to correct, an atom's drop, a nerve-width
distance, molding the moving pattern in air
as we thrust forward at dozens of miles an hour
ever so accurately tuned to pressure, breathing
deeply to bring in joy, breathing surely to keep
all synapses open, to feel with all the skin pores
open, the instant's change, to know precision, I, who...

have lost us in the Maryland countryside on a gleaming
Autumn morning. I am driving through a Breugel
which has turned into a Bosch. Mephistopheles
leads us on, the speed is soaring, at what hill
shall we climb the air, never to settle back
to earth in recognizable form, when will he
make his play to finish the lead he has started,
he with his fresh young face, the hair curling
on his forehead, innocence answered our question,
how do we? where is it? how do we get to?
and he bounded away with us after him, in a race
which turned sinister on a soaring left turn
when we both spoke his name—out of the blue
ice sky: *Mephistopheles!*

> Samuel, do you take this
> road to be the truth?
> There is no truth.
> Samuel, do you take this
> road to be a fact?
> There are no facts.
> They, like people,
> are always changing.

40

2.

At a glass podium, leaning on air,
the Chairman of the Affair,
in caressing voice told the audience there
the thing he should never have said anywhere.
(He had forgotten his covered dish.
he would be the cover if I would be the dish.
All too risky, too risque, such games
we play. Nothing but the liltingest fare,
3 in the sack to two in the classroom,
let's skip the evening do and do. Skip
to my Lou, but where.)
And then he broke the rules and called me friend.
Called me lonely, can't he see I'm not? All
these people gathered around? and he needn't
have said he hoped the poems kept me from being so alone.
There behind a crystal podium, where I couldn't hide.
There behind my transparent poems where I couldn't hide.

Ride out the hurt.
Ride out the fear.
Hurt and fear are always there.
Hurt was a dappled pony
and Fear was a Chestnut mare.

3.

What can a poet do? What can a poet expect to do?
From my dark side comes on Mephistopheles, even
in bright October sunlight, with the sky radiant
leaves brashly making lollipops of the trees,
and Sam beside me, beautiful Sam, anticipating the day.
We aim to stay true to ourselves.

> Ann, there is no truth.
> Sir, is there any self?
> Wrap the words in hard covers
> Display them on the shelf.
> All the cover-ups are hard.

What are you most afraid of?
> *Dying.*
It hangs in my ear like a bell,
> *like our microphone.*

> Brother Sam, I loved it when
> you didn't recognize at dinner
> our host for lunch.
> Sister Ann: Looking out
> from inside this face,
> I think no one will
> recognize me.

> It is not my new clothes,
> Basho, that make me think
> my friends will not know me,
> it is the change from
> love to hate and back again.

4.

And Mephistopheles, wherever you are,
I hope the Maryland cops catch you
doing eighty over the Maryland
countryside before you lure
other dummies (read poets)
toward their demise.
Murder is not suicide,
don't you know anything at all?

Come back, Sam.

Filling in the Blanks

FILLING IN THE BLANKS

Are you now—or have you ever been—
slovenly, lazy, bored, indifferent or
cured? What is your level of pain?
If I barked in your ear all night
would I be a dog or a tree, what
would you be?
Anemic? She was my friend
in second grade, until she cut
the pictures from my books.
Anyone who cuts pictures from
books is a potential murderer.

Message for J B: if I had not agreed
to murder
I might be satisfied
with suicide. I am down on my knees
looking for the o that fell out of
your name. No wonder you turned to
G   D at the end. Dear God. Dear Job.
Dear John,
the letter read. no, it didn't.
it read: My dear, before we make
a terrible mistake, I must tell you
I have found the music to light
my life. She plays piano. She kneels
to God in a Catholic Church. She is tall
and ripples as she walks. She has won
my heart completely. Please return it.
I am sorry to hurt you, but
I would hurt you more if,
loving her, I came back and
married you. You are a fine etc, etc.

My mother ate the letter.
Would she want to know
he was jailed for bribery?
that he failed to reproduce himself?
that he drank himself to death
long after he killed her
driving too fast in his new Hudson,
long after they both had married,
and I with her in the back seat
as she asked him to slow down.

The music-in-his-life arrived today
in a clipping from the Des Moines Register.
At 83, she has no retirement plans,
has 52 piano pupils, diabetes, and
a broken finger from a fall. Once
she offered me her wedding dress
to be married in. If I had not
been wearing my mask of innocence,
I would have told her to go to
her Catholic hell. She was
the definite article in my mother's
grammar book. She caused the misery
that filtered down, smog before we
ever heard of smog, depression
that silted through the tight shut
windows, the heavy air nobody
talked about. So when the Great
Depression came, we were relieved.
At last we could speak up. Blame
somebody. Curse the government.

There ought to be a law. and there
was. Sorry J B but Papa said it first.
I'm plagarizing him, not you.
Were you in terrible pain? Fill
in your loss level. Put in
percentages. Cry. Grandmother
retaliated by saying the nuns wore
white collars to hide their dirty
necks. Put on clean underwear,
you might be in an accident. I was
an accident. Meant to be born
somewhere else. Something else.
I forget just what. I retaliated
by writing a play *You Can't Smell
the Lilies Much* and she heard it
over and over on the radio. It told
where his love really was. It wiped
her out like chalk on a slate. Could
I still hate that old mud-dauber
face? How many blanks will I have
to erase before I can cancel the stamp,
forgive the piano keys. Can you open
a lock? When the locket appeared in
your hand, whose face was in it? If
you had the Hudson at bay, who would
you be? Is nettle a noun or a verb?
Are you ingratiated? Are you
in at all?

THE IMAGE

I have escaped. I hover here
astride this little dollar sign,
this unidentified flying object
in disguise. (want to see

an inside loop?) It's hard to say
just how I got away. I'll try.
Remember when we changed
from daylight saving time?

Somehow I wedged myself in the vacant
hour, and was gone before anyone
knew I was going, even me.

I have always appeared to hover,
so this position is vaguely recognized
as I angle in to those who care
to see me. (I have lost

all fear of quicksand and
the carpenter ants which haunted
my past.) Here I am only concerned
with the taller cement mountains
and updrafts of laughter.

CLASS REUNION

Ring the old school bell,
we are coming home. We cluster
together only a little.
The chance that brought us
into one class was passion
or duty. Born within
the six necessary months,
we were fifteen small colts
to be broken or led to
water and books.

Three can't come back:
one was killed in a war,
one was mashed at the wheel of her car,
one sickened and died of
complications.
The rest of us have died a little.
Could I come out of curiosity?

Correction: our soldier is already there.
The government said yes
so he came home by boat in a box.
(Madame President of
the Alumni Society: It won't
interest you to know
that I speak with him often.
I don't know why, but he turns up in dreams
more often than I can account for.
It won't interest you because
I won't tell you. Because
then you would know I am as mad
as you always knew I was.)

Dear Belle:
I am so sorry. Any
other day but May nineteenth.
I have not seen you all for twenty years.
With God's help I shall escape for still
another twenty.
Love,
if you can,
Ann.

Now I will take a red pencil
and re-vein my heart.

GUSSIE WEARS HER RED SUSPENDERS

Do not touch me with your tongue,
it splinters. Special, you said,
what's so special about you?
        I was tongueless for an answer.
(Pile up bodies like cord-
wood, those who would agree,) but
I am the most special of anyone
in this bathtub. (Don't you believe
in sparrow-logic?)

I might have been pretty once,
but dressed in a long-legged suit of shame,
I never even knew my face was fresh.
I'd catch a glimpse sometimes
of eyes a certain blue.
I'd try on smiles at night.
But looking was a sin.

Skulk under the forsythia bush
...run, run, the japonica bush is near.
Here we lay for half
the night, wrapped in each other's arms.
And he gave me his red suspenders.
(Name? Name? did he have a name?)
Was he even there? Or how did I come
by these red suspenders?
Looking was a sin and I never saw him.

MAD HANNAH

Old Uncle Solemn led her by the elbow
into the parlor draped with felt and floss.
"Mmm..." he mumbled, "I think you ought to know,
something I must tell you..." She said "Yes?"
He was pulling at his bearded face,
she was aching for his phlegmy throat.
"You're a woman now..." but he did not look
to prove it, looked away beyond the Irish lace.
"He's my own brother, but he hasn't any feel
about the way a woman should be treated.
And you can't stay in arm's reach of him, now
our mother's gone." "All right," she said and
touched his arm. He sighed and wiped his forehead
with a handkerchief of red.
    Who would tell him that his message came
    years and years too late?
    Nobody. Nobody nobody.

I WILL HAVE NO IDOLS BEFORE ME

On learning that Charles Lindbergh is dead

Charlie is my darling, my darling,
my darling, oh Charlie is—was
and now he has slipped into that
atmosphere that held him so chivalrously,
until we all could hold him in our arms,
call him brave, enduring and ours.
Charles is a strange name for an idol.

They read, of course they read. Didn't
the Des Moines Register and Tribune come
every day delivered by a knickered boy
being dragged around by a great canvas bag?
sometimes my brother, sometimes my cousins?
Was it my fault the only books in the house
were Horatio Alger and the Tarzan Series?
and (beside my Papa's bed) the Dream Book
and the Bible which were also dare-devil books.

And in that movie house, divided by the royal
light beam down the center aisle, came
all of those hard-riding, hard-loving
heroes, while heroines dressed as Tom Mix
swung from the chandeliers, to knock
out the villain in a double-footed whammy
and my god how we cheered! Was it any wonder

when the choices were actually made,
I decided quilt-making wasn't for me, tho they said
I made the evenest, daintiest stitches
on the block. I didn't want to wake up
in the night forty years later listening
to a train whistle. I didn't even want
to marry the engineer. I wanted to fly
the train.   Ah, Charlie!

FOR GREAT GRANDMOTHER
AND HER SETTLEMENT HOUSE

Over the mantel in the settlement house in Gary,
there is a picture of my children's father. He
is nine months old, sitting on his grandmother's
lap. She is seventy-nine with bristles
on her chin, and a champion heart under that
great round pincushion breast, disguised
as a watermelon.

Grandma said, no no no, but the Sunday class
gave the picture anyway, and I'm glad they did.
Now when we go by Gary we'll stop to see Grandmother,
though she died thirty years ago.
The children will say, looking at the madonna and child,
is that the time you peed in Great Grandmother's lap?
They will admire the Mona Lisa smile on Grandma's mouth;
they know the story well: how she kept on smiling
while the wide-eyed boy on her lap
soaked her right down to her corset. For them
   she is alive, and warm, and wet.

THE SHAPE THINGS TAKE

I take off along the road
gathering wild stones
and blue chicory.
All of the stones are
arrow-shaped and white.
All of the flowers are
daisy-shaped and blue.
I am woman shaped,
blurred.

A horse-shoe print brings back
a flourishing snuffle,
a ruffle of air outside
the dark kitchen. A slam
of screen door starts
a clattering of hooves.
The sound could only come from the big horses.
But that was late last night.
Now only the meadow stretches
green toward the horse fence
and beyond, and the mountains
stretch blue, to blue sky.
There are no horses anywhere.
But their hoof prints, horse-
shoes show raucous on the road.

And horse-shoe prints
focus on a bedroom wall
where Uncle Berge lived, the one

we hid the knives from.
And later, Uncle Hod, the one
we hid ourselves from
after we learned
we had to.

Living uneasy
stiffens the pattern.
Trained for
unhappiness,
you help it happen.
Bullies
are also trained.

THE MOTHER

Of all the scenes she drew on,
it was the one about putting
the bicycle on the airplane
she remembered when she needed
to remember what the children
looked like. Sometimes, of course,
she had to hunt around to find
the children. Sometimes they
would be hiding under the cowling
just to tease her, and sometimes
they would be inside the bicycle
box nailed in and the bicycles
would be chasing her around
the airplane struts, and once
even into the pilot's seat where
the lead bicycle just reared back
and whirled its footpedals
furiously and tossed its handle
bars. It was harder and harder
to find the children and she
was never fully aware when
they all became mute. For
years she could hear them
coming in the side doors yelling
her name MaMa! or theirs, but
now the words she hears are
Robert's home and he was never
one of hers. He was out of
her own childhood and it was strange
how she could reach out and touch him
when she needed to. She never
managed to have him touch her
in return. Rearing bicycles
was the best she could do.

"THINGS ARE STILL COMING ASHORE"

I thought I would be sitting
in a circle of prayer for you,
and maybe this is it, this
solitary circle, after circling
my house to hunt some way
to say goodbye.

        I found
a miniature gardenia by
the front step, flooding the air
with fragrance. Clusters of Fashion
roses by the back door...you made
your own fashion, letting your daughters
change the color near your face.

There was a black butterfly
whispering over the car top,
measuring it for something. Back
and forth...like an old forgetful
seamstress, trying to get the shape
right...was it you?
I am coming apart at the seams, stitch
me, stitch...

        On my bed "The Immense Journey"
lies face down. "Things are still coming ashore,"
says Eisley, "and things are still going into the deep."
And you know that and I know that. Glass angels
fly in my room and crossed on my platter of rocks
are two long pelican bones. What will anyone read
in my palms after I am dead? I only learned
this summer that the lines keep changing.

AND THE TEMPERATURE DROPPING

This winter of '77 puts me back in
those Iowa winters when we wore
our long underwear to bed under
the flannel nightgowns, between
the flannel sheets, piled with
woolen blankets, our feet on
liver-red hot-water bottles and woe
if they leaked. The huge iron cookstove
in the kitchen was our haven, our feet on
the open oven door. The parlor closed off,
even the dining room shut away with ice
forming on the inside of the windows.
The mud ruts in front of the house frozen
solid for weeks on end, the coal supply
for the furnace dwindling. And there by
the old cookstove in the middle of the night
sits Gramma wrapped in blankets, nursing
her elbow that predicted the weather
more rightly than the solemn weatherman
on the Atwater Kent. There she sits
in her wooly slippers, her pointed
nightcap, and her lemon liniment,
trying to rub her club elbow back to
feeling, and it getting colder and colder,
and pneumonia, the Old Man's Friend,
just around the corner.

Danny and I have just come in from walking
the frozen hedge-tops, clumping along in our
galoshes, and on our heads the brown packing
boxes, with slits cut for our eyes.
Somewhere there are planets colder than ours,
but this ice-block night hulks in my memory,
our whole lives frozen ahead of us,
and each knowing we would melt into it,
flowing to another frozen point
that would eventually take us all.

Cleared For Approach,
Cleared for Landing

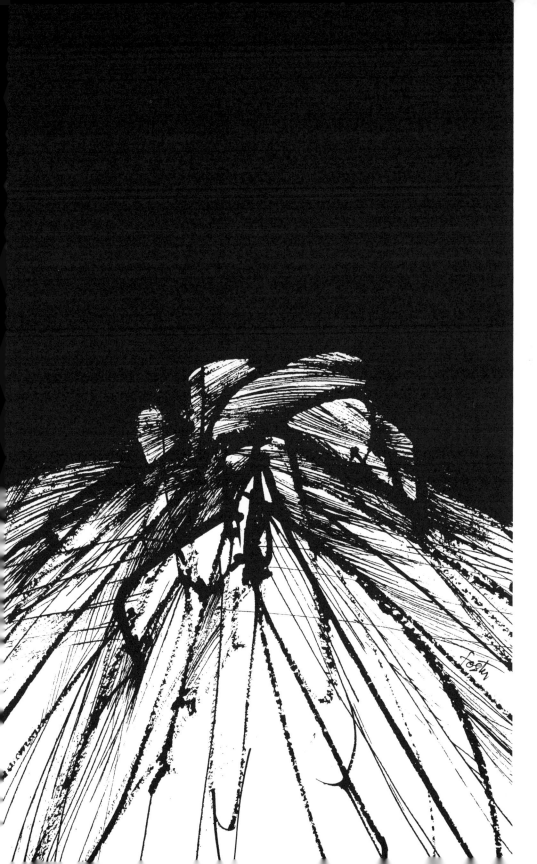

CLEARED FOR APPROACH,
CLEARED FOR LANDING

1.

If you draw the vectors down the middle sky
translating them as you go to wind velocity,
accelerated heartbeat, awakened belief
in a trail of blood, blood on the salt-lick,
blood on the high grass, blood on the oat-trough,
you come to the heaving ram in the field,
a mound of sodden wool, his face torn and hanging,
and the vectors cross in your gut while your eye
catches the skulking sight of the dog turned wolf
slinking away through the trees. The cold sun sinks.
Bobbing lights bring on the veterinarian
to stitch the stricken sheep
before its breath goes out.
Dark overtakes him.

> Was it a slaughtered lamb?
> Were we to make some sacrifice?
> What have we done to this
> mounded meadow, broken some
> wilderness code, pretending
> we are civilized?

514 How do you read?

2.

Through the window above the kitchen sink,
past the log pile stanched between two trees,
past bare branches of dogwood, hickory,
splashing against winter skeletons
is the blare of your red coat and I freeze
with the dishcloth in my hands, freeze
with terror of the familiar.
What do I know that I cannot know?

Once in a movie of clairvoyance,
spilled black ink turned red,
and the father, running,
found only a red coat floating,
all that was left of his own
Red Riding Hood. Your red coat
floats through the trees. I know
you are digging a grave.
I have no clue to what terror floats toward us.

        We move in time as we can.
        The signals always come on,
        they drift into focus and out
        and sometimes in orange-red light
        we see them clearly crossing
        on a blood-soaked woolen coat
        like our own sheep in his field.

        I am wearing my own red coat.
        There is blood on the salt-lick,
        blood on the trough. a low growl
        forms in my throat

514 How do you read?

66

3.

Church time, Sunday morning.
The electricity has gone off,
the sky has come down.
Fog envelops the house,
moves in great clouds across
the meadow. In our eyes the winter trees
come and go, in our ears, the roar
of engines magnifies, too close too close.
Swooping, it comes and goes
and we know...we know.

We know nothing.
The house has turned cold.
We freeze in knowledge
and move on again.
The knowing moves in great clouds across
the meadow, comes and goes.
We do not want to know what we know.

4.

My depth perception melted years ago
as I was hanging clothes, when my fingers
reached beyond the clothesline.
Reach exceeding grasp is no good
in a capsule plane. Accuracy is everywhere
or there is no anywhere.

At eleven 09 on Sunday morning
the plane droned low over our house.
20 seconds later it flew into Weather Mountain.

I am not responsible. I have accurately
figured that I could not have reached
the telephone, called the field, alerted
the crew. The moment of crash is exact.
The speed of aircraft is recorded. Twenty
seconds is not enough time to reach up
my hand in the air and stop that flight.
Now you know who I think I am. And
guilty of everything.

Madness lies
in a route into Weather Mountain.
The Great Observer watching it all,
becoming the Great Not-Quite?
My life passed before me in the middle
of the fog on Sunday morning
and made a bee-line for the peaks.
Flew into a mountain. With all
aboard singing and dancing
and the altimeter working, after all,

68

and the flight path accurate
and the hearing optimal. So what
of the rain and the wind and the fog?
Under that throttle is power, and with
that power we flew into Weather Mountain.

> A head is hanging
> in a tree. Firemen hunt
> for bodies. I wonder about
> the fingerprints when
> the fingers are forsaken.

I am guilty, Jesse Glass, of not replying.
Hallucinations haunt my dreams
and your robed monk disappears over and over
through the wrinkle at the end of night.

514 How do you read?

5.

11:09:55
TWA 514 from Dulles Approach. Tell me your altitude.

11:10:01
Trans-World 514 Dulles. How do you hear?

11:10:12
TWA TWA Five One Four, Dulles Approach. Do you read.

11:10:24
TWA 514 Dulles. One Two Three Three Two One.
How do you hear me?

11:10:30
TWA 514 Dulles. Do you read?

11:10:44
TWA 514 Dulles. One Two Three—Three Two One.
How do you hear me?

11:11:08
TWA 514 514 Dulles Do you read? How do you read?

       Only the fog reads.
       The rain puts out small fires.
       There are several minutes
       up against the mountain
       when only the flames and the fog and the rain
       move. Everything else is still.

6.

LET ME ASK YOU ONCE AGAIN, CAN
YOU CLARIFY

(Can you resurrect? Speak in tongues?
Join the proper arms and legs to the proper torso?)

AS NEAR AS YOU REMEMBER, EXACTLY
WHAT DID YOU SAY AND DO?

(Crawled around the floor hunting the plane,
crawled around my head hunting my last words,
where was the plane, I called and called and
no one answered. I called where are you, he
was right there in my picture, right there
on my slate, I could see him wave, he was right
there, see, there, but he wouldn't call back
to me, he wouldn't even answer, and I told him
allyallyocks in free, but he wouldn't come
and I yelled and hunted him and he wouldn't
come, and for spite he splattered himself
on the mountain. I called him to come home
but he wouldn't come.)
I cleared him for approach.

IS IT TRUE THAT YOU CLEARED THE AIR
PLANE FOR FINAL LANDING?

Oh no. I cleared him for approach. *(I cleared*
him to come home free, allyallyocks, I said,)
I cleared him for approach, not for landing.

WOULD YOU CLEAR UP THE MATTER OF
THE DIFFERENCE BETWEEN APPROACH
AND LANDING?

Approach is coming into the flight pattern,
the necessary flying configuration at a specific
level...

ALTITUDE?

Altitude. *(and you fly that altitude until I say*
you can't. I tell you what to do, and I told him
to come home. Dammit. Why was he coming, anyway?
We weren't expecting him. Why didn't he fly to
Timbuktoo or Baltimore? No one belonged
on that runway. Nobody ever lands there,
it could have grown over with grass and floated ducks
for all we knew. It wasn't fit to fly that day,
even the ducks were walking, as they say, and oh god,
I can't help everything, doesn't anyone realize that?
that the body is alive, oh god, alive alive, ally, alack,
alive's in free, I'm free, I'm free. Why didn't he
come when I called him?)

CAN YOU HELP US CLARIFY APPROACH AND
LANDING?

There's the approach and then there's the landing
approach. *(anybody knows that—it's clear enough—*
anybody knows)

AND IF YOU SAY CLEARED FOR APPROACH DOES
THAT MEAN APPROACH TO THE FIELD OR
APPROACH TO THE GROUND?

It means whatever there is to do next. *(It means*
exactly what it says. You're trying to confuse me.
I'm free you know. I came in frée, I freely came
to testify.) I'll tell you anything you want to know.
What do you want to know?

DID YOU KNOW THERE WAS A MOUNTAIN THERE?

No.

7.

From here you can see the course
the plane took. Huge splintered
trunks stand upright, forming
the shape of the plane.

An icy wind rattles paper caught
high in a standing tree. A small
woodpecker is sending a coded message.

Under my foot is a piece of
pleated fusilage, wedged so tight
under rock, only machines can
dislodge it. Machines have put
it there. Miscalculation has
put it there. Poor communication
has put it there with the horn
blowing and the pilot shouting
GET THE POWER ON. We know because
it is all there on a tape preserved
in a small orange box which records
every sound in the cockpit, in case
we need to know. We need.

The final sound is of the crash.
It is preserved on the tape
in the small orange box.

8.

I have flown
that sloping flight over and over
in my sleep, angling
over the Alleghenies, over the Shenandoah
headed for the building that flies
which Saarinen made for the airport.

Tonight in a wandering sleep I knew
I was not responsible, I *was* the crash.
It was my own inevitable end, to be
splattered on Weather Mountain,
and here I am kissing the ground
and picking up pieces.

9.

It is said that in the FINAL CRASH
by whatever bomb is currently in operation,
Our Government will retrench
at Weather Mountain: the biggest open
secret in the East. There is a marker there
that arrows from the West—a long strip
of match-stick splintered trees—a charred
pointer. Beside that final holocaust
this crash will be but "a drop in the bucket,"
a small flint. We know and we do not
want to know what we know. Everyone
has second sight. We all wear bloody
coats, watching the dog turn wolf.
514 or any other number, do you read?
            How do you read?

10.

And then it was I heard the horn
blowing through fog, and I did not cry
out, but gave all power and rose up
and cleared the mountain and the weather

and knew all that was left to me.

Ann Darr, born in Bagley, Iowa, graduated from
University of Iowa, went to New York City
where she wrote and performed radio scripts for
NBC and ABC. As a pilot during World War II
she flew with the Woman's Airforce Service Pilots
(WASP) in the Army Air Force, testing planes at
an advanced trainer base, towing targets in B-26's
and flying mountain mapping missions.

She has won the Samuel LeFevre Speech Prize, a
Discovery 70 award from the Poetry Center in
New York City, and a National Endowment of the
Arts Fellowship 76-77. Two collections of her
work have appeared, *St. Ann's Gut* and *The Myth
of a Woman's Fist,* from Wm. Morrow & Co. She
has recorded for the Library of Congress
Contemporary Poetry Series and, for Watershed
Tapes, *High Dark,* a selection of her poems.

She has three grown daughters, lives with her
husband near Washington, D.C. and on a farm in
the Blue Ridge Mountains.

Drawings and book design are by Susan Foster.

Cleared for Landing has been composed at The
Writer's Center (Glen Echo Park, Maryland) in
English Times, a typeface based on Stanley
Morison's Times Roman. Twenty-five hundred
copies have been printed for Dryad Press by
Dulany-Vernay, Inc. (Baltimore). Fifty copies have
been bound in boards, numbered and signed by
author and artist.

27.

Ann Darr

Susan Foster